/ SENSE OF PLACE /

It is a term we use often, and for good reason.
As designers, we are ultimately building an
experience. Our process starts with a conversation,
which leads to a vision that takes shape through
creativity and collaboration. The spaces that
we create become meaningful when they evoke
memories, and cultures, and context and connections. What turns space into place? The same
passion that turns ideas into movement: a funda-
mental drive to create environments where people
connect. It's the difference between a sense of
belonging and merely passing through. It's also
how we work together to bring our ideas and
buildings to life. Strange and wonderful things
happen in the space between our client and team
collaborations. There is curiosity and discovery
and questioning and the sheer magnitude of
shared experience. Sometimes we wander; other
times we roam. But we always arrive together –
on common ground – in a much more powerful
place than the space from which we started.

IDEAS + BUILDINGS
2010 / VOLUME .03

This book is for everyone.
Any of us. All of us.

You.

Anyone who believes that
ideas and buildings can honor
the broader goals of society.

Start somewhere that excites.
Open it at the middle.
Or the page second to last.

Begin anywhere.

That's where the best ideas
come from.

75

PERKINS
+WILL

The first steps that Larry Perkins and Phil Will made were to take a very conscious approach to deeply consider the human occupants of the building in a way that results in innovative architecture.

Phil Harrison, Chief Executive Officer

/ INNOVATION GENERATION / **Phil Harrison**

The life of our firm is made up of many stories—of architects and designers, ideas and buildings, spaces and places—and every story has a beginning. 75 years ago, Lawrence B. Perkins and Philip Will, Jr. founded Perkins+Will on a vision and set of core values that continue to guide us today. From our roots laid down in the Midwestern Plains, we have grown from city to country to continent and back again, helping to shape our world and transform our profession as a whole.

Since 1935, Perkins+Will has been built on the strength of our talent and our relationships. Together, we have grown the firm through the quality of our work, the passion of our team and our commitment to honoring the broader goals of society.

Today, we are designers of the world. Our team numbers more than 1,600 passionate professionals who have worked in countries across the globe. Our continued growth is a result of our commitment to our mission. We have diversified the services that we offer our clients, expanded our areas of practice and refined the expertise that was evident the day we broke ground at Crow Island School. As one of the world's largest design firms with 23 offices globally, our portfolio of high-performing projects across civic, education, healthcare, government and private-sector clients sets an extraordinarily high mark.

We think bigger about who we are and what we offer. And to help sustain our lead, we have continued to focus on educating our professionals to design structures and built environments that harmonize locally—conserving resources and preserving local ecosystems, promoting the health of occupants and unifying communities through design. We continuously strive to evolve our practice and improve how people live, work and learn. Because we believe that if we can help improve the health of our minds, our communities and our planet, everything else follows.

Yet even as we have evolved, the legacy of where we came from endures through our shared experiences and collective achievements—through our collaboration, creativity and trust, and through our shared commitments to modernism, sustainability and evolution. Since our founding, these themes have inspired and driven us and are there to see in everything we do. We continue to collaborate with our clients to create places from spaces, helping to express a shared vision while enhancing the lives of our clients, communities and society at large.

Today, we're the largest sustainable design firm in the world, but we're still the same architectural firm at heart. This is our legacy, and this is our future.

A COMPACT HISTOR[Y]

1935
LAWRENCE B. PERKINS
AND PHILIP WILL, JR.
FOUNDED "PERKINS+WI[LL]

'38 P+W hired b[y]
Winnetka Public S[chool]
along with Eliel S[aarinen]

'41 P+W of[fice]
located
Mercha[ndise]

'44 sch[ool]
market[ed]
in

'47

'36 with a new partner, the firm became "Perkins, Wheeler & Will"

'39 during early years, designed over 50 houses, many in north suburbs

'42 earlier offices were at 333 N. Michigan and at 225 N. Michigan

'45 PRINCETON PARK housing and BENJAMIN ELECTRIC CO. in Des Plaines

'48 Larry Perkins very much involve ... speaks, writ

'51 manu MINNEA GALE

1940 com compl3 and

'43 P.W for

'51 Accepted several houses including Trip in E

...ols ...nen

...es the ...se Mart

...o are a growing ...RUGEN SCHOOL ...view is completed

...st staff structural engr. ...total staff = 23 people ...es for year = $230,000

1950 new structure = "The Perkins & Will Partnership."

First high school = BARRINGTON

3 KEOKUK H.S. in Iowa ...illion dollar bldg ... Arch. Fore...

EACH
PERSPECTIVE
WONDROUS
THAN

PERSON'S
IS MORE
AND COMPLEX
THE NEXT.

1953 / Low gables, wide eaves and the prow-shaped form of Heathcote Elementary School in Scarsdale, New York, reflect the influence of the Prairie School and the philosophy that pervaded progressive education at the time.

/ COLLABORATION / **Put some kindling on the flame.**

In the beginning, there were two. Two friends who came together out of mutual respect and a passion for doing great work. We shined our first light by designing houses and steadily moved on to other commissions—doctors' offices, churches and schools. Soon, new opportunities stoked. The big beacon, Crow Island School, became the groundbreaking collaboration that would set the standard for how we worked on projects moving forward. To truly innovate, we place our clients' interests at the center of the flame: we had to walk in their shoes, dream what they dream and make their challenges our solutions. So we set off on a trail—together with our clients—of dialogue and discovery. Our capabilities expanded. Strategic partnerships blazed. Today, no matter how complex the project or how many disciplines involved, one thing does not change: we ignite ideas and buildings that reflect our client's mission and community. From our schooling on Crow Island to our collaborations across continents, ours is a culture fueled by constant conversation. We ask questions. We listen. By arriving together, we burn even brighter through a journey of collective sparks.

CAN, AND
BETTER
SOCIETY.

1968 / Located in Connecticut, Stamford Hospital
expresses a smart sophistication and daring in its
curved façade and clean lines, reflecting the health
and well-being of American Modernist design.

/ MODERNISM / **Create environments that lift people's spirit.**

When the world thinks of Modernism, a few famous ideas rise to the top: less is more, form follows function, ornament is a crime. To the casual eye, Perkins+Will buildings are modern by these standards. But our true modernist core goes beyond a certain design style. More than anything else, we are modern in our belief that ideas and buildings can, and should, better society. This approach inspires everything we do and every environment we create. Our work aims to improve the living standards of our people, our clients and everyone they reach. These are the principles that Larry Perkins and Phil Will established when they founded Perkins+Will. It's what they believed then, and it's how we practice today. A look back over our 75-year history reveals all types of projects. But the heart of our work lies in our commitment to advancing the way the world designs, builds and uses environments to improve how people live, work and learn. It's our personal commitment to create solutions that contribute to human well-being and enhance the long-term health of our planet.

Architecture really is about placemaking. It's about analyzing the place where the building is going to go, and then having the building add to that sense of place, or create a new sense of place within the existing content.

Ralph Johnson, Design Principal

Education comes to its senses.

School break. For Perkins+Will, our big break was Crow Island School. In 1938, Perkins, Wheeler & Will won the commission for a new elementary school for the Winnetka School Board in suburban Chicago which had originally been called Southwest Elementary School. Superintendent Carleton Washburne recognized Larry Perkins as an ideal man from whom he wanted design input, but his Board felt the young firm needed more experience to complete the job. Led by Larry, the architects persuaded Saarinen to associate with and contribute to the project. The commission was signed, and an idea was born. For months, Larry Perkins went to school, observing Winnetka's progressive educational program in practice. Day after day, from bell to bell, Perkins studied the teachers and students, jotting and sketching in exchange for the occasional story. Suddenly, designing a school meant becoming a student.

Completed in 1940, Crow Island rose from the class of its contemporaries and attracted national attention. The low-slung, flat-roofed, one-story structure of beige brick and pine was set in informal gardens and represented an entirely new approach to the design of an elementary school. Crow Island quickly became a pioneering model for the modern American school and has influenced school design in America and around the world ever since. In 1971, The American Institute of Architects, recognizing architectural design of enduring significance, chose Crow Island School as the recipient of its 25-year award.

Ahead of the class. Larry Perkins had been a student of his father, Dwight (1867-1941), who was an accomplished and recognized architect of schools and civic spaces. Before his son, Dwight Perkins had been an innovator in school design and planning, having been a draftsman for Burnham and Root and working alongside Frank Lloyd Wright and some of the leading architects of his day.

Dwight Perkins was a strong proponent of natural light and ventilation, enlarging school corridors and stairways in order to ease congestion. He also was a proponent of what today seem obvious renovations of the school plan: integrating toilets on every floor. The details made the difference. In effect, Perkins let the light into schools at a time when Nelson Algren described Chicago as "the dark city." Over the course of his career, Dwight Perkins designed more than 40 new schools in the Chicago area and across the Midwest, helping lay the foundation upon which his son would build.

BREAKING THE MOLD / L-shaped classrooms broke from the traditional, neo-classical mold and help to create multi-use spaces perfect for learning.

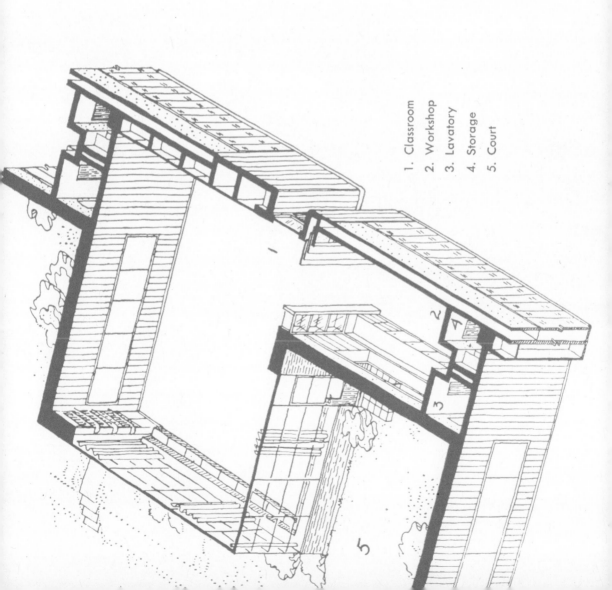

1. Classroom
2. Workshop
3. Lavatory
4. Storage
5. Court

Modern sensibility. What was so remarkable about Crow Island was that Perkins saw the school as a tool for learning. Crow Island was the first school to be zoned by age groups. It reflects in plan an important insight into the life of the child. Primary pupils cannot comprehend the complex social structure of a school community of 300 to 400 students. The team followed that logic to create classrooms that worked as self-contained units, or pods, that contained everything except the library, playroom, offices and auditorium. As Bill Brubaker recalled the idea of those pods, "It's just the idea of breaking up the space into smaller, more adaptable, more personalized spaces." The design revolutionized the school by making it fit for the life of the grade school student.

In their work at Crow Island, the firm came to realize a simple, but powerful, truth: the grade of our schools affects the grades of our students. The life of our buildings affects the life of our minds. As Larry Perkins wrote, "A beautiful building is one that is sensitive to the emotional needs of the people who use it, and one that serves the physical functions set for it, and one that has been designed with the understanding of the

materials and methods it requires." Architects of the mind, Larry Perkins and Phil Will documented their research from Crow Island, passing along a legacy that would educate generations of architects and designers. Later, Larry Perkins wrote two books on school design and planning, *Schools* (1949) and *Workplace for Learning* (1957). As Larry Perkins would later recall as the driving force for the vision of the firm:

"An ideal of an architecture that derived beauty from a sensitive response to need was a beacon we held before ourselves. We believed that the most direct use of structure was automatically graceful – hence beautiful. We called it "functional." We were only partially right. We had to learn that logic was not enough – that preconceived design mannerisms were not enough. We have had to learn over and over again that the analysis of our day, and the computer of today must be subordinated to concepts that will lift people's spirits."

MIND'S EYE / The classrooms, home for students throughout the day, provide a sense of safety and security with access to the outdoors. An expanse of windows in every room offers uninterrupted views and a feeling of unlimited possibilities.

Innovation as the crow flies. For Perkins+Will, the success and recognition of Crow Island led to subsequent commissions that helped to establish a vital practice. After World War II, the Baby Boom fueled demand for more elementary schools, which, in turn, resulted in more commissions for the firm. As the Boomers grew, so did Perkins+Will. The firm graduated from a practice focused primarily on elementary school design to a wider range of projects, including high schools, colleges and universities.

Since Crow Island, a love of learning and a user-centered design approach have come to characterize the work of the firm. Through its 75-year history, Perkins+Will has been recognized for overcoming challenges in educational environments through architecture and design. The firm's recognizably fresh and modernist designs — low, informal, rambling buildings in wood, brick and glass — are attuned to the natural environment and the needs of the students, faculty and community.

Schools are humble buildings in many ways. They need to be cost-effective, durable, efficient and respectful of their

communities. Finding inspiration and vision in these environments is as challenging as any other design problem. Education is constantly evolving, with our world and our schools becoming more and more complex. Teaching and technology are forces that have merged and continue to change and adapt what role the built environment plays in the educational process. Perkins+Will continues to receive awards for school design and has come to be recognized for a humanistic approach to architecture and for creating schools that were well-suited to the student.

CHILD'S EYE / Crow Island was designed through the eyes of its students. Door handles, blackboards, cabinets and light switches were scaled to the childrens' height, and auditorium seating was graduated from shortest to tallest, giving each student a front-row seat. Whimsical sculptures designed by Lily Swann, Eero Saarinen's wife, conjure child-like imaginations and adorn the school's walls.

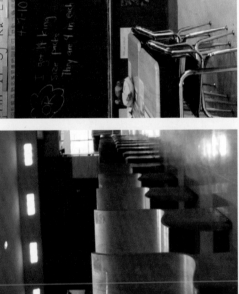

In 2009, Perkins+Will partnered with DeKalb County Schools to concept Sprout Space, a new breed of sustainable portable classrooms. With its agile anatomy, natural light and cost-conscious materials, Sprout Space won the Relocatable Classroom category in the Open Architecture Challenge. The exposure helped seed new funding to turn the page on dreary trailers and pioneer Sprout Space as a universal and smart solution for tomorrow's classrooms.

PROJECT / **Sprout Space**   CLIENT / **DeKalb County Schools**   TIME FRAME / **One month**   PERKINS+WILL / **Atlanta**

Allen Post / John Poelker / Shawn Hamlin / Jack Allin / Joe Jamgochian / Sumegha Shah / Erika Morgan

BLACK

Portable classrooms have become part of the landscape of overcrowded and underfunded schools. They are basically black boxes — single-wide trailers with few or no windows, poor air quality and bad acoustics. Kids hate them, teachers cope with them. Although meant to be

BOXES

temporary solutions, these dingy and dim receptacles routinely stay in schools for five years or more. There are more than 300,000 in the U.S. alone. Every year, the quality of these classrooms degrades, leaving students in the dark. Our kids are boxed in, and they're being boxed out.

I ALWAYS END UP FREEZING ONCE I COME IN THE ROOM.

SOPHOMORE, DRUID HILLS HS

SENIOR, DRUID HILLS HS

THEY'RE TRAILERS. DON'T CHURC IT UP

LIGHT

Natural light can be a powerful architect of change. Studies show that the addition of daylighting techniques to students' surroundings can boost concentration, test scores and even attendance rates. Students with limited classroom daylight were outperformed by those with the most natural

LABS

daylight by 20% in math and 26% in reading. Using daylight makes spaces appear larger and helps conserve energy. Opening up the classroom to the outdoors empowers students to explore their dreams. The first lesson of Sprout Space begins with a simple principle: Illuminate to animate.

"Look with all your eyes, look." *Jules Verne*

GIVE
STUDENTS
ROOM TO
EXPLORE,
EXPERIMENT,
FAIL,
LEARN,
GROW.

MAKE LEARNING SPACES FLEXIBLE TO ENGAGE DIFFERENT MODES OF TEACHING

"The whole building is a teaching tool." *Allen Post, Team Manager, Sprout Space*

School of thought. Maslow's hierarchy of needs tells us children need to feel safe and secure before they're even ready to learn. Kids are natural-born scientists and tireless explorers. Give them a sunny spot to take root and sprout.

A moveable feat. Sprout Space is designed to go anywhere, adapt to different environments and reconfigure on a dime. Daylight, dynamic spaces and a recyclable afterlife are lessons for the day.

INCUBATE. ILLUMINATE.

Taking its cues from nature, a Sprout Space module mimics this simple form. Opening along its seam on both sides, singular or multiple pods can be configured to adapt to different environments.

THINK OUTSIDE THE BOX.

Learning becomes transparent from the outside in
through abundant windows and communal gardens that
double as outdoor classrooms. Exterior whiteboards
are both a teaching tool and billboards for legal graffiti.

BREAKOUT. BREAK THROUGH.

Active areas to engage and display work help to trigger the senses, arouse curiosity and stimulate learning retention. An outdoor patio serves as a teaching garden where children can grow.

LEEDer OF THE CLASS.

Sprout Space is built with sustainable materials:
FSC certified wood, high-reflective roofing, bio-based
insulation and flooring, a butterfly roof rainwater collection
system and ample daylighting to conserve energy.

SQUARE ROOT OF MANY.

A square plan offers students similar sight lines and easier access to the head of the class. Sliding walls give teachers more flexibility in configuring desks and tables.

01 PV PANEL
02 INSULATED PANEL ROOF
03 STEEL FLITCH BEAM
04 ALUMINUM STOREFRONT SYSTEM
05 FIBER CEMENT PANEL RAINSCREEN
06 WRITEABLE SURFACE
07 INSULATED PANEL WALL
08 BIOBASED FOAM INSULATION
09 TUBE STEEL
10 WIDE FLANGE LONGITUDE BEAM
11 ADJUSTABLE HEIGHT PIER
12 METAL PANEL RAINSCREEN

01

02

03

04

05

06

07

08

09

10

11

12

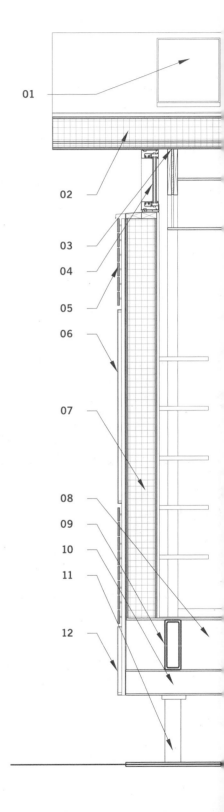

A LIFE'S WORK / The firm has helped raise generations of architects and designers, who often became life-long friends and mentors. A culture of collegiality and camaraderie still pervades all of the offices of Perkins+Will today.

EVERYTHING IS
CONNECTED

TO EVERYTHING ELSE.

1967 / The National Center for Agricultural Education, Research and Extension, set in Chapingo, Mexico, was Perkins+Will's first international commission and translates Le Corbusier's influence in its freestanding piers.

/ SUSTAINABILITY / **Sustain the sustainable.**

Perkins+Will has always been interested in treading lightly on the earth. While we've long taken the lead on sustainable design, we welcome the challenge of sustainability as a huge opportunity. It's not enough to lead today. We have to lead for tomorrow by taking a holistic approach to sustainable design. This means sustainability in how we operate, create and inspire others. We were the first design firm with a national reach to commit to the 2030 Challenge, pledging that all of our projects be designed for carbon neutrality by the year 2030. More recently, we've started to develop tools that help

the design industry achieve this challenge as well. And that's just the beginning.
Sustainable design is an organic process. We test, experiment, learn and revisit. We explore
ways to deliver increasingly diverse projects with the same resources established
by conventional buildings. We use technology to court the natural world, not beat it into
submission. The green movement is ever-evolving and vigorous in our work, with
a spectrum of ideas and techniques. As our work becomes more diverse and complex,
our collective responsibility to a more sustainable future grows.

BREAK-
THROUGHS
THROUGH

TAKE PLACE HONEST CONVERSATION.

2003 / Set in the rich urban environment of Chicago, Skybridge epitomizes the clear-sighted height of high design while bridging humanism with modernism and making its residents feel right at home.

/ TRUST / **Get permission to do amazing things.**

How do you build trust? In today's climate, trust gets a lot of attention, but it's never been a foundation we can afford to take for granted. Everything we do is built on trust. Our buildings affect the way people work, learn, create and play. It is no small responsibility. Of course, only our clients can really speak to why they trust the practice of Perkins+Will. In the end, the subtle dynamics of trust are a feeling more than anything else. For our part, trust paves the way to more productive

and rewarding work. We engage from the outset, and when the challenge gets bigger,
we regroup and rise to meet it. If we are demanding of ourselves, we are
equally demanding of our clients. Trust inspires energy, energy inspires creativity
and creativity inspires the results. It's a level of transparency that comes around full circle
through openness, honesty and accountability. That's how we build trust.
And that's how we aim to keep it.

Our future is a world where human design and occupation of buildings and communities result in the restoration and nourishment of natural ecosystems, and we live in harmony with the rich and fragile biosphere that sustains all life.

Peter Busby, Design Principal

In 2008, an interdisciplinary team led by Perkins+Will's Washington, DC office partnered with the non-profit Arlington Free Clinic (AFC) to design an environment that provides accessible health care with dignity to low income, uninsured individuals in Arlington County. Since occupying their new space, AFC has seen an unprecedented demand for care. The number of individuals seeking to become patients doubled in its first year.

PROJECT / **Arlington Free Clinic Interior Design** CLIENT / **Arlington Free Clinic** TIME FRAME / **Fourteen months** PERKINS+WILL / **Washington, DC**

Tama Duffy Day / Jonathan Hoffschneider / Jamie Huffcut / Lori Geftic / Rachel Conrad / Matthew DeGeeter / Richard Adams / Marian Danowski

SOCIAL

For the residents and local communities of Virginia, the prognosis was grim. The U.S. Census Bureau reported that an estimated 1,025,400 Virginians were uninsured for all of 2008. According to the Virginia Health Care Foundation, in 2007, Virginia ranked 48th among all states and the District of Columbia in Medicaid coverage of low-income adults between ages 19-64, making

FABRIC

Virginia the third-highest state in uninsured citizens. While disparities in income and access to healthcare were increasing, the gap between the haves and have-nots was as well. The need for affordable access to healthcare was clear. Solutions to increase access to high-quality care impacted not only the health of Virginia's residents but also the fiber of the state's communities.

Healthy start. Through academic partnerships with Texas A&M University, George Mason University and Roanoke College which guided behavioral mapping, observation, focus groups, graphic surveys, literature review and pre- and post-occupancy evaluations, the planning and design of AFC was informed by qualitative and quantitative data and evidence-based design.

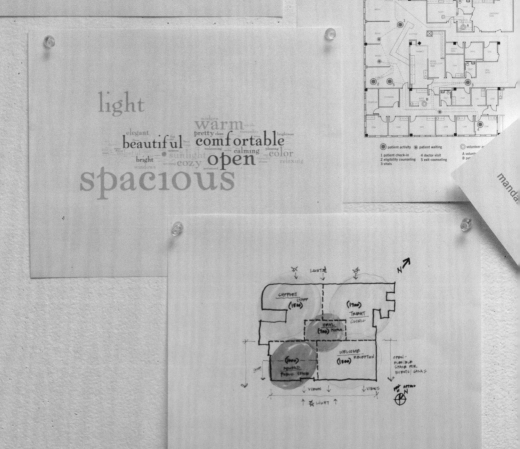

KEY WORD.
RESPECT
DIGNITY
SAFETY
COMMUNITY
QUALITY
EFFICIENCY

STYLE "WOW!"
LIGHT
COLOR
SUSTAINABLE
WAYFINDING

Culture of care. AFC is Perkins+Will's first project that embarked on a process of creating generative space—a place both physical and social that increasingly improves over time. This process focuses on improving human health through research and the design of an environment resulting in individuals, organizations and communities that flourish.

Proving that design can be sustainable and affordable, AFC incorporates sustainable features throughout, all within the mandate that project costs not exceed five percent the cost of traditional design elements. A free clinic built entirely from donations, the clinic was an investment in the health of the community and the planet.

FLOWER POWER / The research and generative space process led to a solution inspired by a flower. The core symbolizes AFC's life-enhancing and systemic mission, while the petals illustrate the components of AFC: welcome (reception and waiting), treat (medical and behavioral healthcare), support (staff and fundraising services) and community (educating and engaging patient and volunteer communities).

WELCOME
TREAT
SUPPORT
COMMUNITY

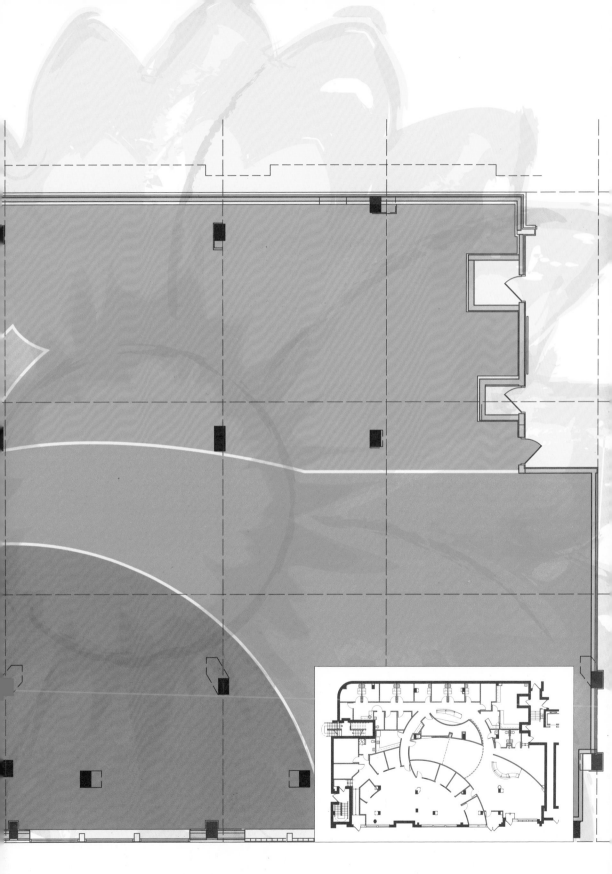

Picture of health. Through the Social Purpose Initiative of allocating billable time to pro-bono work, Perkins+Will and Bognet Construction participants transformed a clinic corridor into a showcase honoring AFC's 500+ volunteers. From floor to ceiling, magnetically-mounted photos of the clinic's volunteers capture the community support that is at the clinic's heart.

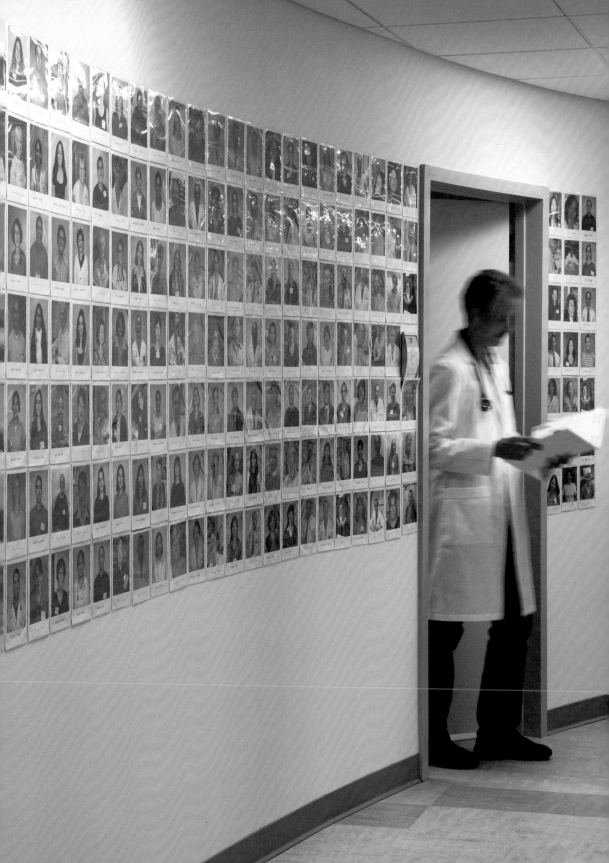

WARM RECEPTION / In a post-occupancy survey of the Clinic's staff, all of the respondents reported that the new space is light-filled and uplifting and three-fourths said that the new space inspires health.

100%

RESPONDED THAT THE NEW CLINIC SPACE
IS LIGHT-FILLED AND UPLIFTING.

79%

THOUGHT THAT MORE COMMUNITY ACTIVITIES
AND EDUCATION WILL OCCUR AS A RESULT OF
THE NEW CONFERENCE SPACE AREA.

75%

INDICATED THAT THE NEW SPACE
INSPIRES HEALTH.

First-born. Arlington Free Clinic is the first free clinic in the country to achieve LEED Gold certification and the first LEED Gold certified medical facility in Arlington County. AFC has been recognized through several awards, including the Washington Business Journal's Green Business Design Award, Healthcare Facilities Symposium National Team Award and a Special Merit for Sustainability from the International Interior Design Association, Mid-Atlantic Chapter.

Sleight of hand. A conference, education and activity space is accessible through a series of curved, sliding and folding doors.

Bright ideas. Recognizing the benefits of natural light, an open interior plan allows for shared daylight, improving health.

Pillars of the community. Dynamic structural columns were left exposed, creating a unique and recognizable rhythm throughout.

On the surface. Well-specified interior materials along with strategically placed hand sinks reduce the spread of infection.

Stress-tested. Design attuned to patient and practitioner needs increases satisfaction, evokes calm and instills a sense of well-being.

Body language. Design elements of the project, including the pattern language and lighting, help shape an environment designed to heal.

Designed to meet the Living Building Challenge, the new Visitor Centre at VanDusen Botanical Garden has an eye on the future. Perkins+Will, collaborating with internationally-renowned landscape designer Cornelia Hahn Oberlander, has set its sights on creating a green facility that will flourish within the ecology of the surrounding gardens. Together, the new facilities and gardens will create a focal point for the city of Vancouver and a place where creativity will run wild.

PROJECT / **VanDusen Botanical Garden Facilities Renewal**   CLIENT / **Vancouver Parks Board**   TIME FRAME / **Three years**   PERKINS+WILL / **Vancouver**

Peter Busby / Jim Huffman / Harley Grusko / Penny Martyn / Paul Cowcher / Jacqueline Ho / Matthieu Lemay / Robin Glover

The site of the VanDusen Botanical
Gardens has had many lives. Once
an area that lay dormant, the land
was owned by the Canadian Pacific
Railway and was used as a golf
course, leased to the Shaughnessy
Golf Club in 1911.

EVOLUTIONARY THEORY

When the Railway proposed
developing a subdivision on the
land in the 1960's, a group of
citizens opposed the decision and,
working with the Vancouver Park
Board, protected 55 acres for the
site of the Gardens today.

The Gardens were later funded
by the City of Vancouver, the
Government of British Columbia
and the Vancouver Foundation with
a donation by W.J. VanDusen,
after whom the Gardens are named.

Planted in a prominent area of
Vancouver, the Gardens are
set amid rolling lawns, tranquil
lakes and dramatic rockwork.

Despite being surrounded by
neighborhoods, there was a lack
of awareness by many residents
about the Gardens. The new
design needed to find a way to
make the Gardens, facilities
and residents all feel at home.

MAZE

In the West, we were once settlers on a new frontier. What lay ahead was wild: a natural world that was unruly, untamed and uncontrolled. Nature was dangerous and hostile so we used brute force against its forces. Nature became public enemy number one. And in our rush forward, we became control freaks—plotting, and planning and pruning our spaces to keep nature out

HAZE

and always in check. But our ambition blinded us and we lost our way. We devised mazes of cities and towns that kept consuming our natural resources. There was no end in sight. Our consumption seemed unavoidable and soon, unstoppable. Over time, this approach

I DREAM OF GREEN CITIES WITH GREEN BUILDINGS WHERE RURAL AND URBAN ACTIVITIES LIVE HARMONIOUSLY.

Cornelia Oberlander, *Landscape Architect Consultant*

OUR VIEW OF THE FUTURE IS THAT THE SEPARATION BETWEEN HUMANS AND NATURE WILL DISAPPEAR.

BLUE

With the evolution of regenerative design, we're opening our eyes to nature and our relationship with it. We're finding new beauty in its powers, and we're seeing the need to integrate our plans with its processes. The focus on our planet alone has broadened to consider how populations evolve and grow. Conquer becomes collaboration. Nature becomes nurture. Green fades to blue.

EYED

We're creating new ways to build symbiotic and sustainable relationships with our environment. Inextricably-linked and inexplicably-beautiful, the Gardens and facilities bear the simple truths of good design and a sustainable and regenerative approach: Everything should fit together. Everything should flow together. Everything should work together.

Leaps and bounds. By defining the highest standard for sustainable design, the Living Building Challenge provides a way to push past our current bounds.

Conceived by Jason F. McLennan and unveiled at Greenbuild in 2006, the Living Building Challenge is a set of benchmarks and tools for architects and designers to achieve the highest level of sustainable design possible. Just as LEED helped to define earlier goals for green building, the Living Building Challenge pushes LEED targets, setting challenges that today have yet to be achieved. At its core, the Challenge encourages and helps educate designers to balance the needs of both the natural and built environments.

The Challenge works like nature: it takes something complex and interconnected and focuses all its energy on something absolutely pure in its purpose. Nothing's wasted. Everything's needed. All of it's real.

The Challenge gets us thinking. It gets us moving. And it gets us closer to a sustainable future.

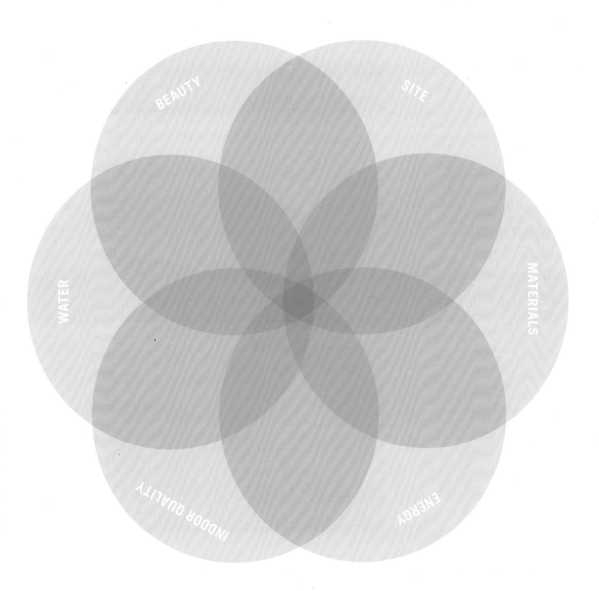

EAST

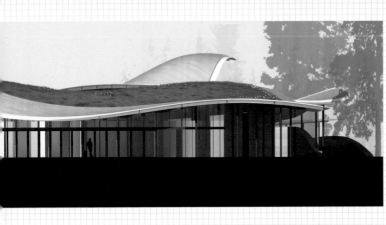

WEST

Form fits function. The design of the Visitor Centre combines art and science in a perfect modern vision. Through its cultivated and regenerative approach, the space creates a place that can heal the natural environment.

EYE OF THE BEHOLDER

Stop and stare. The building's central atrium is illuminated by a 12-sided glass and steel oculus. Lit by sun and stars, you can see the future of regenerative design.

Inhale. Exhale. As sunlight heats the air in the interior, the inclusion of a perfectly-sculpted, perforated-metal element accelerates the exchange. The heated air rises and escapes through the vented roof. And the process begins again.

Alive and well. The roof blooms from the building's center, providing a focal point, luring nature in while letting air out.

Craftsman. Ship. By opening up the design approach to the craftsmen and construction teams earlier in the process, VanDusen exemplifies building a team from the ground up.

BOTANICAL GARDEN

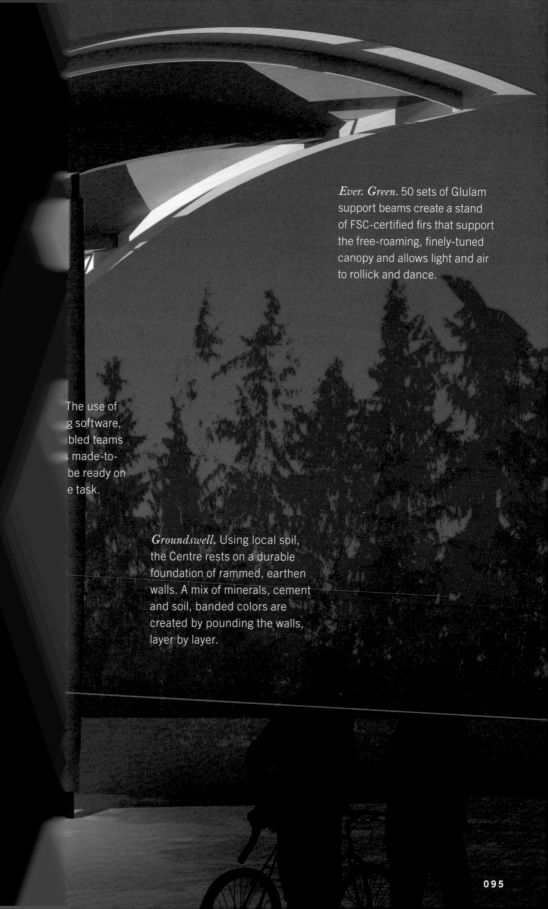

Ever. Green. 50 sets of Glulam support beams create a stand of FSC-certified firs that support the free-roaming, finely-tuned canopy and allows light and air to rollick and dance.

The use of
g software,
bled teams
s made-to-
be ready on
e task.

Groundswell. Using local soil, the Centre rests on a durable foundation of rammed, earthen walls. A mix of minerals, cement and soil, banded colors are created by pounding the walls, layer by layer.

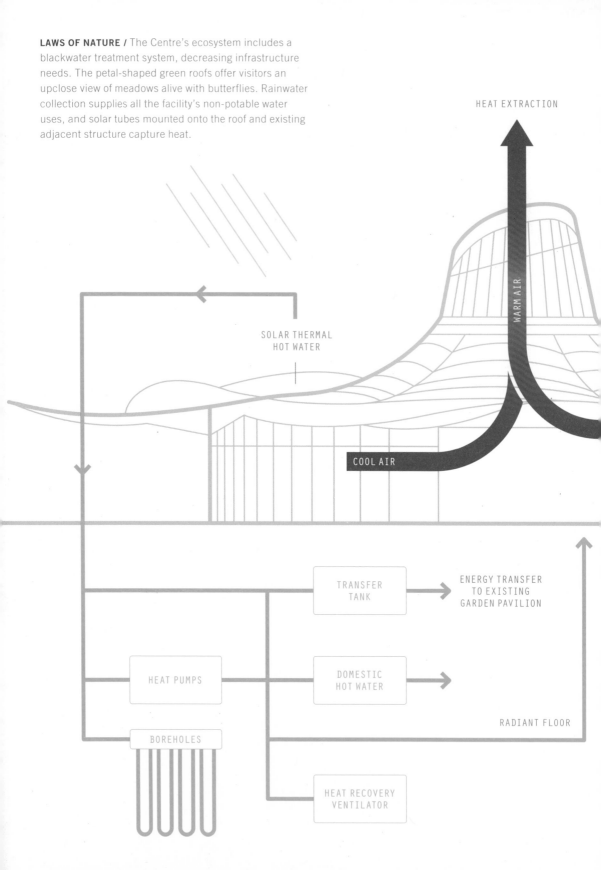

LAWS OF NATURE / The Centre's ecosystem includes a blackwater treatment system, decreasing infrastructure needs. The petal-shaped green roofs offer visitors an upclose view of meadows alive with butterflies. Rainwater collection supplies all the facility's non-potable water uses, and solar tubes mounted onto the roof and existing adjacent structure capture heat.

HEAT EXTRACTION

WARM AIR

SOLAR THERMAL
HOT WATER

COOL AIR

TRANSFER
TANK

ENERGY TRANSFER
TO EXISTING
GARDEN PAVILION

HEAT PUMPS

DOMESTIC
HOT WATER

RADIANT FLOOR

BOREHOLES

HEAT RECOVERY
VENTILATOR

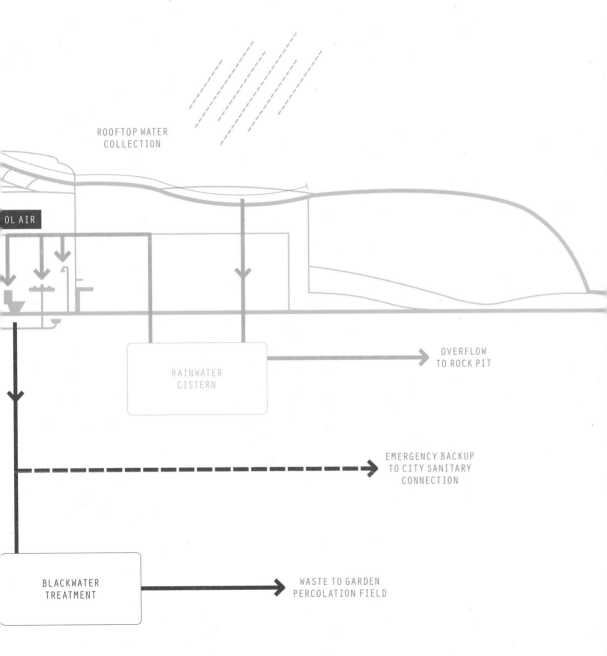

ROOFTOP WATER
COLLECTION

OL AIR

OVERFLOW
TO ROCK PIT

RAINWATER
CISTERN

EMERGENCY BACKUP
TO CITY SANITARY
CONNECTION

BLACKWATER
TREATMENT

WASTE TO GARDEN
PERCOLATION FIELD

VOLUMES OF LEADERSHIP / Whether found in user-centered research practices or interdisciplinary approaches to design, the firm's love of learning has made their team architects of the mind, creating a rich legacy for generations to come.

97

The St. Clair High School was built in 1927 at a cost of $194,000. A grant enabled the shows a suite at cost per cubic foot of 38 cents. I remember at per cubic foot of $1.00...

THE WRONG
IS THE
IN SEARCH

ANSWER RIGHT ANSWER OF A DIFFERENT QUESTION.

1963 / Edens Theater in Northbrook, Illinois was a landmark visible along Chicago's Edens Expressway. The futuristic theater's concrete and curved roof pointed sharply upward, putting a dramatic and fine point on the style of the period.

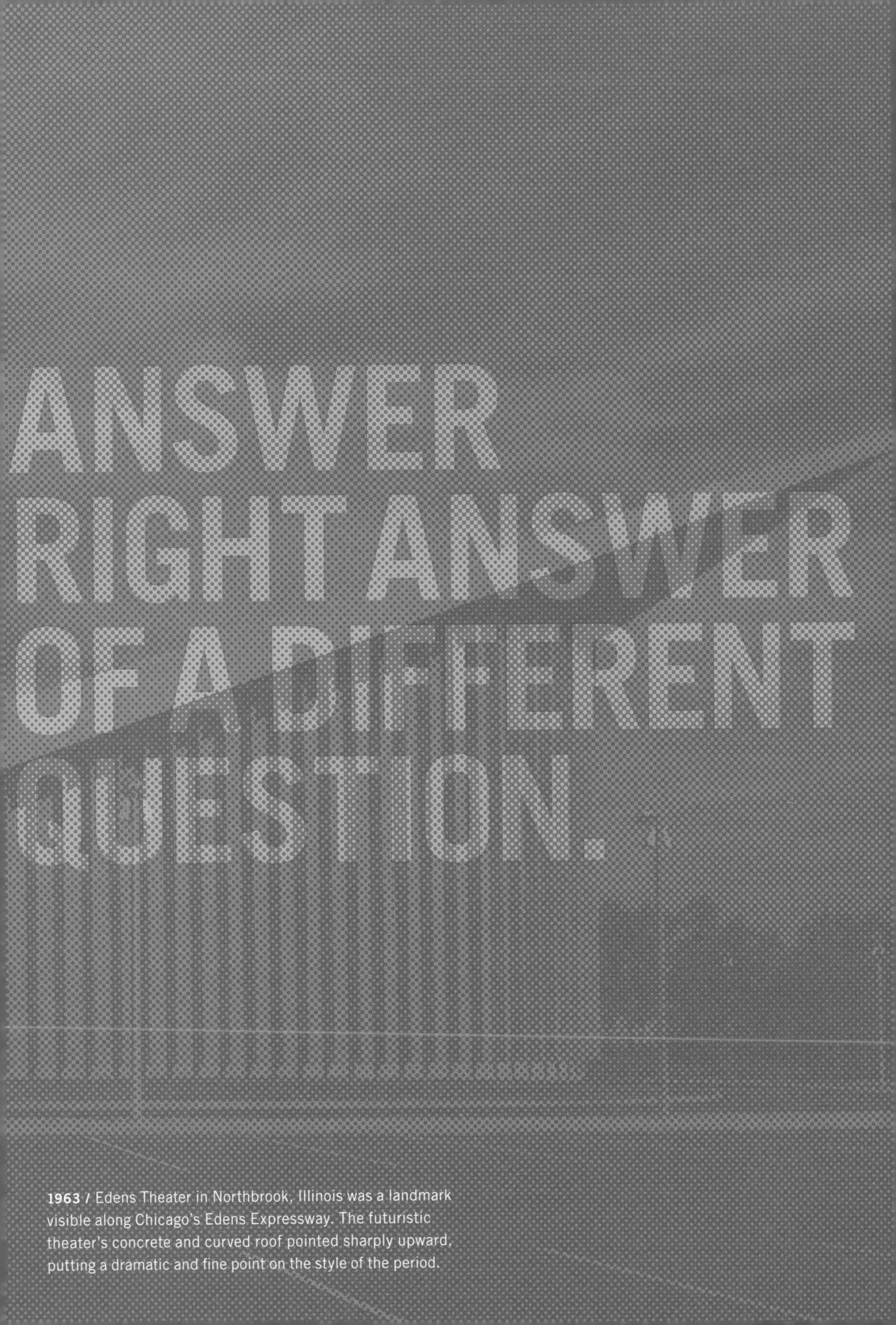

/ CREATIVITY / **Take an everyday idea and make it true.**

One might say that the real aim of creativity is to point the way to the truth. Great ideas can come from anywhere. Over the years, Perkins+Will has worked tirelessly to tap into our reservoirs of creativity and problem solving to create momentous change—from our first big break to our next assignment abroad. To solve problems, you have to remove yourself from the process and become the person for whom the work is being done. What makes us creative is how we explore new possibilities for everyday uses. There's room for both tradition and innovation in what we do. Let's question the assumptions and see whether there is something new we can try. The surprises can help create the context of right now. Therein lies the beauty of modernism for so many unique projects and disciplines. It's understanding the rituals that take place and relating them to our ideas and buildings and not being afraid to take risks. Our ability to trust our instincts, break with tradition and reinterpret proven methods has fueled our growth. We use imagination, curiosity and critical thinking to discover and innovate. Not that we don't like to have fun. That's part of the process.

WE THRIVE
WE ARE
POSSIBILITIES
TO BE

WHEN OPEN TO AND WILLING TRANSFORMED BY THEM.

1993 / Recognized by the AIA for its design, The International Terminal at Chicago's O'Hare Airport has become one of the world's hubs of travel and transportation and a hallmark of the evolution of our jet-setting age of globalization.

/ EVOLUTION / **Be an agent of change.**

The old adage is true—if you don't know where you're going, how will you know when
you get there? You have to do more than embrace change—you have to learn
how to evolve and survive beyond a lifetime of experiences. Over the years, Perkins+Will
has grown from an American architecture firm into a global, interdisciplinary
leader of design, architecture and environments. We built our foundation on education
and healthcare and rapidly expanded to a wide range of client types in multiple areas
of practice. In recent years, we've grown in new areas such as

Branded Environments, Planning + Strategies and Urban Design. Today, Perkins+Will has completed thousands of projects in multiple countries and in every climate around the world. We are united by our diverse skills and a passion for finding new and innovative ways to help communities thrive. No great achievement comes without obstacles, but we face the next 75 years with the lessons of the past, the courage to take risks, the drive to pioneer and the joy of learning something new each and every day. And working together, the future looks bright.

Space encompasses opportunity for activity.
But place helps to build and shape culture.
Space reflects the culture of an organization
through the contrast of textures, the contrast
of places and ideas where people come together.

Eileen Jones, Global Branded Environments Discipline Leader

The Atlanta BeltLine was born from the collaboration of public, private and grassroots efforts to revitalize the city through a sustainable urban design renewal. Perkins+Will, working alongside James Corner Field Operations, has taken the lead on the design of the BeltLine's Corridor, around which the urban core will grow by as many as 100,000 people. With an aim to improve quality of life and increase mobility, the BeltLine is helping Atlanta get back on track.

PROJECT / **BeitLine Corridor Design**　CLIENT / **The Atlanta BeitLine Inc.**　TIME FRAME / **Two years**　PERKINS+WILL / **Atlanta, Chicago, Vancouver**　CO-DESIGN LEAD/ **James Corner Field Operations**
Leo Alvarez / Ryan Gravel / John Threadgill / Chad Stacy / Kevin Bacon / Jeff Williams / Valdis Zusmanis / Heather Alhadeff / David Green / Micah Lipscomb / Xue Phyllis Zhou /
Matt Malone / Zhen Feng / Zan Stewart / Maxine Coleman / Justin Cooper / Cassie Branum / Nat Slaughter / Eva Maddox / Eileen Jones / Tom Boeman / Lisa Coghlan Dolan /
Kimberly Lindstrom / Lynette Klein / Pamela Steiner / Sara Ahrns / Martin Nielsen / Aaron Knorr

REUSE

At the heart of the project is the addition of a 22-mile transit system that will link residents and riders to the hubs of Atlanta. The design of the BeltLine has re-imagined a new use for a loop of once-abandoned railroads (termed "Belt Line" in the mid-20th century) that encircle the city and will reclaim more than 6,000 acres of urban land. By connecting existing and proposed

RECLAIM

regional transit systems, the BeltLine will create more than 33 miles of multi-use trails and connect Atlanta's neighborhoods, business districts and destinations. The project encompasses the development of green spaces, trails, transit and civic spaces. The project is not only changing the look of Atlanta but also the way that residents see themselves.

Tour de force. The BeltLine sets in orbit a system for how cities can create affordable, sustainable and livable environments. Its urban plan rejuvenates as much as reinvents. The BeltLine will be a conductor of culture and commerce with needed infrastructure to support the life and growth of the city. Fueling the exchange of ideas through open civic spaces, the project will create a centrifugal force of change.

Line of force. For Atlanta, the BeltLine is becoming a powerful architect of change and is helping solve age-old urban challenges in a wholly new approach. Addressing long commute times, poor air quality, auto dependency and limited green space, the project is helping reverse urban sprawl. On the start of its journey, the BeltLine will connect the neighborhoods and communities of Atlanta while helping to support the city's economic development efforts.

WE NEED STRATEGIES THAT ENCOURAGE SMART DEVELOPMENT LINKED TO QUALITY PUBLIC TRANSPORTATION THAT BRING OUR COMMUNITIES TOGETHER.

TODAY, I HAD THE OPPORTUNITY TO WITNESS FIRST-HAND HOW LOCAL PLANNERS IN ATLANTA ARE DOING JUST THAT BY LINKING NEIGHBORHOODS TOGETHER

© 2008 Google

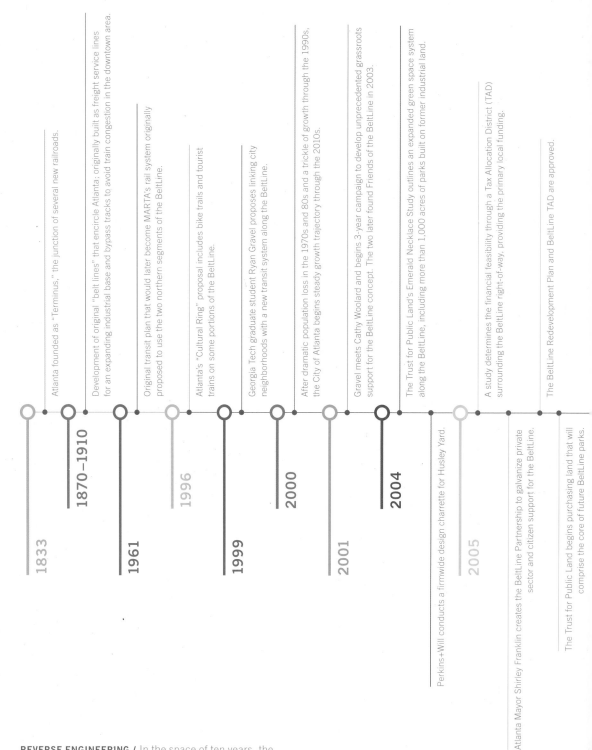

1833
Atlanta founded as "Terminus," the junction of several new railroads.

1870–1910
Development of original "belt lines" that encircle Atlanta; originally built as freight service lines for an expanding industrial base and bypass tracks to avoid train congestion in the downtown area.

1961
Original transit plan that would later become MARTA's rail system originally proposed to use the two northern segments of the BeltLine.

1996
Atlanta's "Cultural Ring" proposal includes bike trails and tourist trains on some portions of the BeltLine.

1999
Georgia Tech graduate student Ryan Gravel proposes linking city neighborhoods with a new transit system along the BeltLine.

2000
After dramatic population loss in the 1970s and 80s and a trickle of growth through the 1990s, the City of Atlanta begins steady growth trajectory through the 2010s.

2001
Gravel meets Cathy Woolard and begins 3-year campaign to develop unprecedented grassroots support for the BeltLine concept. The two later found Friends of the BeltLine in 2003.

2004
The Trust for Public Land's Emerald Necklace Study outlines an expanded green space system along the BeltLine, including more than 1,000 acres of parks built on former industrial land.

Perkins+Will conducts a firmwide design charrette for Husley Yard.

2005
A study determines the financial feasibility through a Tax Allocation District (TAD) surrounding the BeltLine right-of-way, providing the primary local funding.

The BeltLine Redevelopment Plan and BeltLine TAD are approved.

Atlanta Mayor Shirley Franklin creates the BeltLine Partnership to galvanize private sector and citizen support for the BeltLine.

The Trust for Public Land begins purchasing land that will comprise the core of future BeltLine parks.

REVERSE ENGINEERING / In the space of ten years, the BeltLine has helped reverse the direction of a half-century old approach to urban planning that has taken a toll on the health of Atlanta's neighborhoods and environment.

BeltLine Timeline

2006
- To oversee implementation of the BeltLine, Atlanta BeltLine, Inc. is created.
- BeltLine Transit is awarded $1 million in Federal Transit Authority funding.
- The BeltLine Network, an alliance of organizations with an interest in the planning, development and maintenance of the BeltLine, is formed.

2007
- Perkins+Will expands its services with a design discipline in Urban Design and Landscape Architecture.
- Master planning for the 10 BeltLine Sub Area Plans commences.
- 21 acres are assembled in Southeast Atlanta for the development of Boulevard Crossing Park.

2008
- The Metropolitan Atlanta Rapid Transit Authority (MARTA) approves the 22-mile loop alignment and a rail mode of transit as the BeltLine's Locally Preferred Alternative.
- The northeast corridor becomes the first segment of the BeltLine transit corridor to be acquired by Atlanta BeltLine, Inc.
- The first segment of BeltLine trail opens in West End.
- Ground is broken for the first BeltLine park.
- First BeltLine TAD Bonds are issued, totaling $64.5 million.
- The BeltLine Partnership's $60M capital campaign is 50% complete.

2009
- BeltLine Affordable Housing Trust Fund approved by City Council and initially capitalized with $8.8 million in TAD Bond proceeds.
- The BeltLine Affordable Housing Trust Fund launches.
- City Council adopts the first five Sub-area Master Plans.

2010
- Construction on Historic Fourth Ward Park Phase I starts.
- Eight miles of interim hiking trails open on three segments of historic railroad.
- Art on the BeltLine, a temporary public exhibition, opens with more than 40 works of art.
- Perkins+Will, along with co-design lead, Field Operations, is selected for the design of the BeltLine Corridor.
- Planned groundbreaking on the first primary section of trail.

MAGNITUDE OF CHANGE / BeltLine's promise for Atlanta—
in sustainability, connectivity and mobility—is enormous
and could become a model for other cities.

ATLANTA

SAN FRANCISCO

CHICAGO

BOSTON

NEW YORK

ACCESS

SINGLE FAMILY
RESIDENCE EDGES

DEVELOPMENT

PUBLIC AND
PRIVATE ADJACENCIES

PARKS

HYDROLOGY

TREE COVERAGE

SOLAR ORIENTATION

HISTORIC RAIL
SEGMENTS

RAIL + MARTA

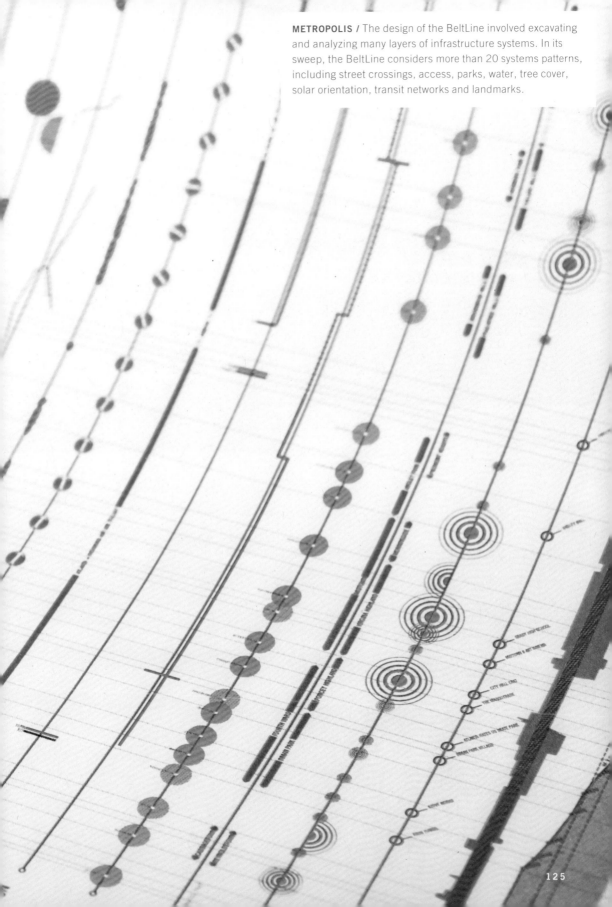

METROPOLIS / The design of the BeltLine involved excavating and analyzing many layers of infrastructure systems. In its sweep, the BeltLine considers more than 20 systems patterns, including street crossings, access, parks, water, tree cover, solar orientation, transit networks and landmarks.

NETWORK / Facilitating the transformation of 45 historic neighborhoods, the Corridor Design unifies typologies for the transit system, trail and their supporting infrastructure of stairs, ramps, wayfinding and signage.

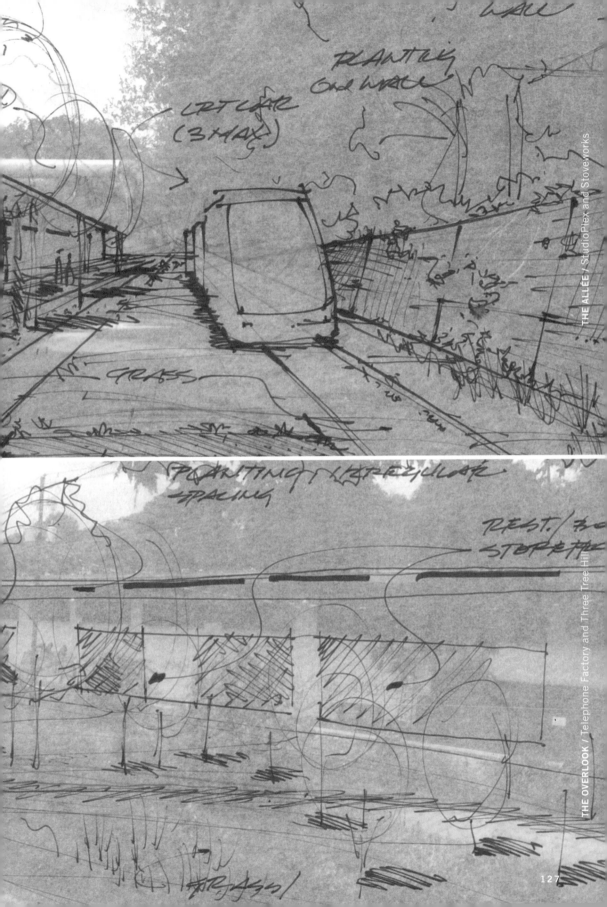

THE ALLÉE / StudioPlex and Stoveworks

THE OVERLOOK / Telephone Factory and Three Tree Hill

STRONG CHARACTER / Taking cues from historic and physical nuances, site-specific planting concepts, spatial articulation, artful lighting and public art provide an exciting sequence of experiential landscape variety, or character rooms.

Drawing on multiple resources from around the world, Perkins+Will collaborated with their network of partners to launch whitespace.bz, an inventive brand for a modern-day way of doing business. Working with their client, a leader in the design and manufacturing of carpet, Perkins+Will created an online carpet business—a toolkit piled high with applications and colored with the richest customer care features in the house. whitespace.bz is keeping step with the fast-paced industry while changing its course.

PROJECT / **whitespace.bz**   CLIENT / **The Dixie Group**   TIME FRAME / **One year**   PERKINS+WILL / **Chicago**

Eileen Jones / Brian Weatherford / Nicole Pallante / K.J. Kim / Lynette Klein / Elizabeth Mohl / Kayo Takasugi

BLANK

In our modern odyssey of exploration, we built cities from towns that have grown to become metropolises that reach as far as our eyes can see. We have circled the globe and opened up a whole new world of possibilities. As we have run out of space to explore, we have begun to create virtual ones, built from thin air. And on the wide open canvas of what could be, we've tried to

SLATE

create what should be: communities that connect, places that inspire. And sometimes, we have left something behind. We have lost something in translation. In much of our technology-driven online communities, thinking sometimes becomes split from feeling. The online world can seem somehow off: right standing apart from left, virtual from vital, real-time from real-world.

More handprint. Less footprint. Our challenge was to equip interior design professionals with a space to browse samples, research specifications, request quotes and make design choices—anytime, anywhere. The result was a place that delivers an engaging experience and a streamlined approach, eliminating much of the inefficiencies of business as usual.

To achieve this, we designed a virtual community that supports all of the functions of a traditional, offline carpet business while providing all of the benefits of digital. whitespace provides an accessible and sustainable environment that eliminates the need for much of the material resources consumed in offline operations—from travel and transportation to retail showrooms and printed communications.

BRAND

B R A N D
POSITIONING

ABACUS →
EXCEL

B R A N D
ANALOGS

APPLE

TARGET

ebay

GAP

MINI COOPER

CRATE + BARREL

BP

APPLE

B R A N D
ATTRIBUTES

AGILE

LAUNCH
STRATEGY

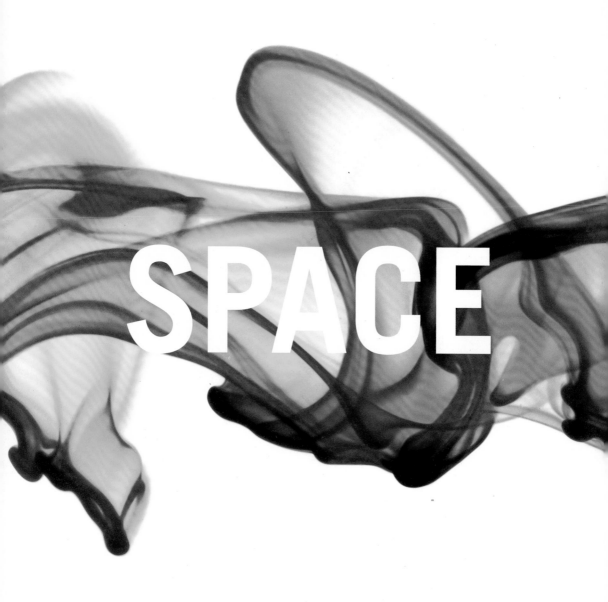

SPACE

Modernism has taught us that imagination can take us virtually anywhere, and that progress begins when you know which way to go. We're creating whole new online environments in which to work and live. When well-designed and well-built, these communities bridge real-time with the real-world in a powerful and personal way. Through an interdisciplinary approach, businesses

RACE

such as whitespace have created places that foster new ways to communicate and new types of commerce. And digital communities support new kinds of culture and vibrant communities. The result is faster connections between thought and action and stronger connections between people and place. Space becomes place. And the race is on.

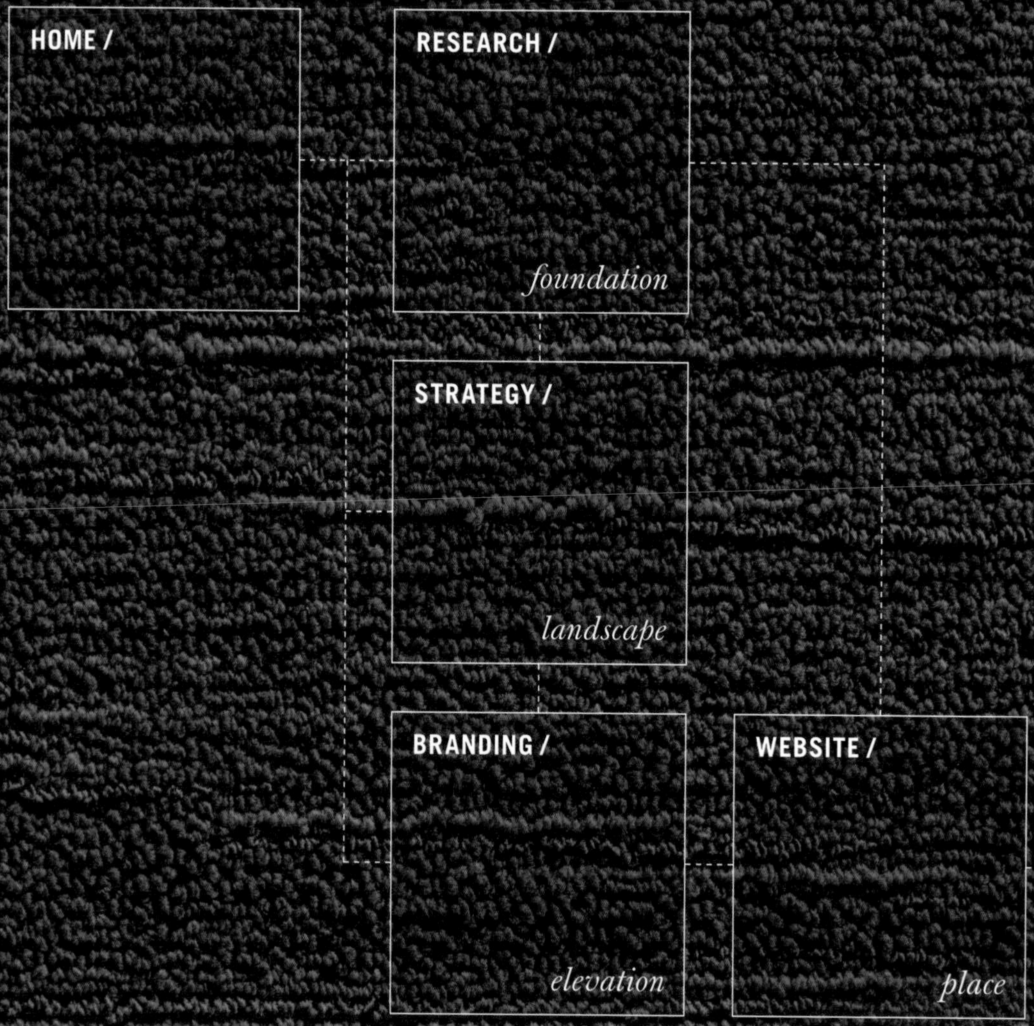

HOME /

RESEARCH /

foundation

STRATEGY /

landscape

BRANDING /

elevation

WEBSITE /

place

PRODUCT /

materials

PHOTOGRAPHY /

details

ADVERTISING /

color

PACKAGING /

texture

Sum of the parts. The scope of the project encompassed 2-D, 3-D and virtual space design as well as the design of the product, brand communications and facilitated customer training. Clean, concise and true to form, whitespace was drawn with an eye to the user in the tradition of American modernism. With a collaborative approach, the opportunities for imagination, innovation and transformation are virtually endless.

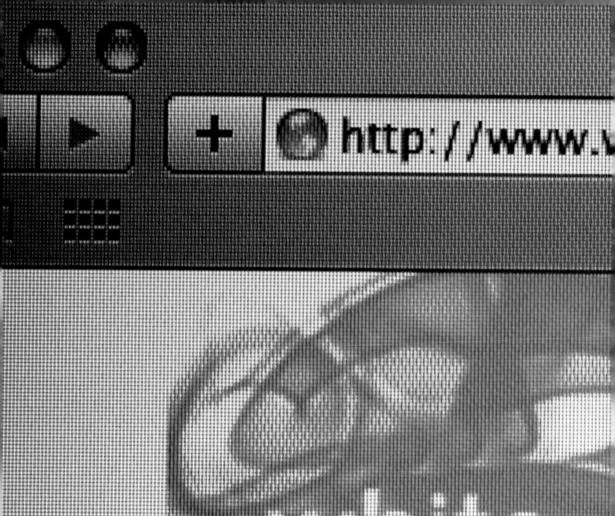

Product

tespace.bz/ws/

ace

Pulse   Techr

whitespace

warp | 8G221

PATTERNS OF THOUGHT / To weave the talents of its practices, the firm conducted a two-day charrette, combining the ideas and energy of product, interior and graphic designers, and architects with strategists and technologists.

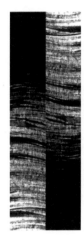
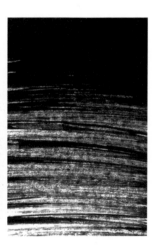

FRIENDLY
AND EFFICIENT
IN DESIGN AND
FUNCTION,
WHITESPACE
MAKES OUT
OF DATE,
OUT OF THE
QUESTION.

EILEEN JONES, GLOBAL BRANDED ENVIRONMENTS DISCIPLINE LEADER

WHITESPACE OPENED MINDS TO NEW APPROACHES TOWARD COMMERCE AND COMMUNITY, AND IN THE PROCESS, HAS OPENED NEW OPPORTUNITIES FOR ARCHITECTS AND DESIGNERS.

OUT OF THE BOX / whitespace packaging integrates
the online experience with the tactile world of interiors.
Simple, smart, shoebox-sized packaging minimizes
material and fulfillment costs while lessening impact
to the environment.

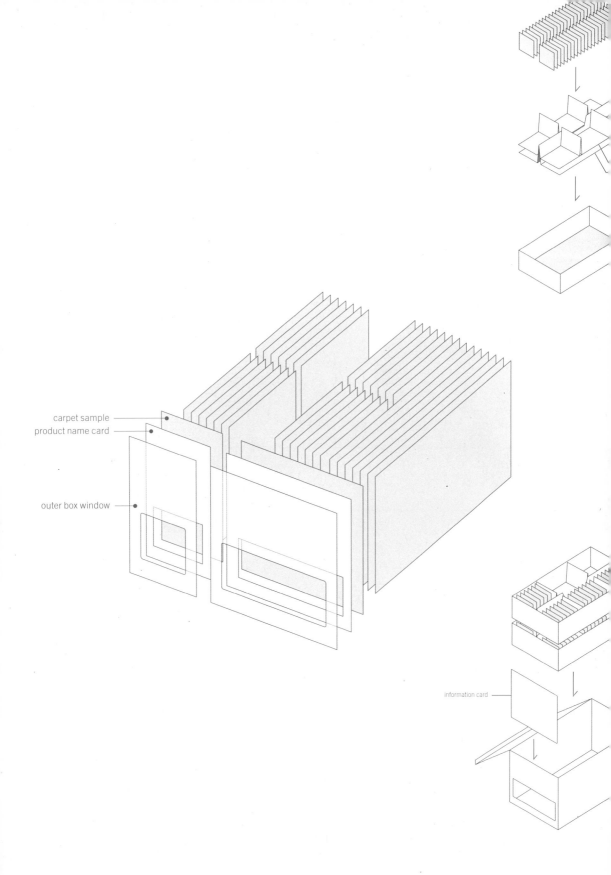

carpet sample

product name card

outer box window

information card

Architecture and brand are synonymous.
Each communicates with us to establish place,
convey meaning or express emotion. We can
walk into spaces and feel good about either
working, living or playing there.

Eva Maddox, Design Principal

Student of the world.

Shape of things to come. Our work at Crow Island was groundbreaking in its approach to the design of a space and how the built environment can become a place for shaping our communities. From the ideas that first took form at Crow Island, our firm would build and grow. Today, Perkins+Will has completed thousands of projects for some of the world's most diverse and esteemed educational institutions with one goal in mind: create spaces that educate and inspire. In the words of John Dewey, an advocate of progressive education and a contemporary of Crow Island, "Education is a social process. Education is growth. Education is, not a preparation for life; education is life itself."

Studies abroad. Located in Riyadh, Saudi Arabia and designed to be constructed in three years, King Saud bin Abdulaziz University for Health Sciences (KSU) is a study in the design of a modern and progressive center of education. Like Crow Island and the generations of education facilities that have preceded it, the design of the expansive campus is grounded in a deep and studied understanding of the students. It is a school of the future rooted in the past, connecting tradition with technology, climate with culture, time with place.

The wadi, the Way and the garden. Settlement of the city of Riyadh can be traced to the natural landform and presence of two branches of the regional waterways or "wadi". The metaphor of the wadi as a wellspring of knowledge has become a source of inspiration for design, and when combined with the idea of "Sharia", as the Way or the law, has formed the overarching philosophy for the Riyadh Master Plan. The heart of the Riyadh academic campus, located atop an existing wadi, forms an interconnected community of spaces that focus on a single unifying garden plaza. Wadi is the Arabic term traditionally referring to a valley; in some cases, it may refer to a dry riverbed that contains water only during times of heavy rain. As the second major circulation artery, the wadi is formed by a series of gardens and paths that meanders on a North-South axis. The design is based on a water formation and will either incorporate a water element or a dry riverbed. In addition, a series of "inverted wadis" (berms) will add depth to the landscape design. The Way is an imposed order on the site that organizes special functions and features on an East-West axis. Acting as one of two major circulation arteries, the Way is an easily identifiable and centrally located corridor aligning the heart of the campus with two mosques. At the core of the Way is a strong and formal allee of date palms and prominent lighting that distinguishes it from the rest of the site.

PATH TO PROGRESS / The meandering garden paths of the North-South axis, representing the wadi, connect the educational zone of the colleges to the healing zone of the hospital.

The exterior limits and boundaries of the Way will be influenced by each district through the use of pavement patterns, site furnishings, smaller plantings and minor water features. The Way and the wadi meet in the premier location of the KSU site, the center of the Academic core. At this location, a combination of large event spaces, smaller gathering spaces, major and minor circulation routes, water features and shade structures forms a clean but complex system accommodating a series of programmatic requirements. Gardens are sensitively located throughout the site to align with major and minor program elements.

World class. For Perkins+Will, the challenge was to create a sustainable and modern space attuned to traditional cultural and religious norms. The result is a center dedicated to the advancement of medical knowledge, research and practice. At 11 million square feet of built environment situated on 2,000 acres of land, KSU is a state of the art hospital combining 200 Adult Specialty beds and 350 Children's beds, a Medical University campus comprised of seven colleges and an administrative complex, BSL 3 research and teaching

laboratory centers, housing, recreational facilities, two Biobank facilities designed to support research by storing up to one million DNA samples, and three Mosques. Form and function are intertwined throughout the facility on an unprecedented scale. Drawn from offices across the firm, the project team was tasked with integrating authenticity and functional flexibility. The design of the space draws inspiration and metaphor from Arabic culture and architectural forms.

DEGREES OF INNOVATION / From top to bottom: The central plaza of the campus at the intersection of the axes forms the heart of the university — a space for student gatherings and ceremonial events such as graduation. Patient drop-off in front of the King Abdullah Specialist Children's Hospital. A view of the hospital.

part in reversing a pernicious feature of history. Building a company that acts as a kind of technology bridge from the developed to the developing world reverses the flow of value. We are bringing new technologies to the developing world – helping to build up their industries and infrastructure and improve the quality of life for their people." Education can do that. Design can do that. And on an unprecedented scale, KSU does that, helping create a world-class facility and a destination for medical sciences, research and care.

Best practices. Set within the harsh environs of Saudi Arabia's extreme climate, the design of the campus captures a garden oasis or paradise, a sense of place connoted by the meaning of "riyadh." Pedestrian bridges and covered drop-offs link an elevated, landscaped medical plaza atop public parking to the medical complex entry lobbies. The horizontal and vertical circulation through the plan establishes the template for the building configuration. The first four ground floors form the diagnostic and treatment chassis that supports the upper bed tower floors. At the lower levels, the floor plates pull apart and recede at the upper floors, allowing for pockets of space and natural light to filter down to the lower levels. The building configuration also serves to shield much of the sunlight at the recessed lower levels. Along the perimeter of lower floor chassis the exterior takes on a much more solid expression. The upper floors of the bed tower hover above an interstitial mechanical service floor which is shielded by a combination of fritted glazing and sunscreens. Campus-wide strategies for LEED Gold certification, aimed at energy savings and efficiency, inform the landscape and urban plan for the Research Center within the Technology District.

Throughout 75 years of design innovation, Perkins+Will has found inspiration and vision in communities, cultures and climates around the world in order to solve challenges for a diverse range of clients. Along the way, the firm has adapted to regions and geographies and discovered advantage in their differences. Together with the firm's clients, partners and communities, the firm has created new opportunities by building spaces that serve the broader goals of society. As the firm has evolved, the thread of our culture perseveres: these are the values of humility, honesty, optimism and graciousness that are more relevant today than ever before.

Since our founding, we have grown from a Midwestern, American practice to a global interdisciplinary architecture and design firm. For us, every project begins with dialogue and discovery. By traveling and growing together, we never extinguish an individual voice but burn brighter through a journey of collective sparks.

King Saud bin Abdulaziz University for Health Sciences will become a global destination for academic medical research and care. At KSU, students and regional research and practitioner communities will share a space that provides the freedom to explore and discover. Students can transition from private to public space as they unveil a world of opportunity through educational advancement graduating to new interests, new ideas and new opportunities. In big and small ways, KSU, lets the light in.

The bridge. As a part of the Dar Group, Perkins+Will is fortunate to have a strong relationship with Dar Al-Handasah (Shair and Partners). Our collaboration on multiple largescale projects, such as KSU, across the globe has been successful for both firms. Dr. Kamal Shair, founder of Dar Al-Handasah, wrote about the work of Perkins+Will, "In a sense, I feel that we have played a small

The following is an excerpt from Phil Harrison's acceptance speech, delivered at the 2010 National Building Museum Honor Award gala in Washington, D.C.

Perkins+Will has received a National Building Museum Honor Award for our commitment to civic innovation in design, construction and education, marking the first time an architectural firm has been a recipient of the award. We truly appreciate the National Building Museum as an advocate for the social relevance of the built environment and we feel a sense of common purpose. In particular, this year's theme of "Civic Innovation" converges with our own aspirations for the future. Our hope is that this recognition not only reflects on our past contributions, but will be a launching pad for our future and, more broadly, a new vibrant age for design and the built environment. We believe that we are living at the advent of an Age of Meaning. In this new era, design will grow in civic importance, as society embraces the transformative power of good design. This will be a time where a renewed respect for the human condition and the natural world will fundamentally change the way we think about the environments we occupy.

Buildings will not simply be less wasteful: we will design regenerative buildings that heal their environments and occupants. Curiosity will be the fuel of research-driven design practices, resulting in innovations that transform the way we use space. Progressive urbanism will redefine the way people connect to place and to each other. Instant access to information will define new levels of accountability and performance. Global mindedness will continue to expand, as geographic boundaries diminish. This will not be a frightening future where technology takes over and the world becomes a generic commoditized environment. Rather, new levels of connectedness, compassion and consideration will lead to a future of lightness, transparency and well-being. We receive this award with much appreciation and with these most sincere hopes for the future.

Today, Perkins+Will is a design firm practicing regionally with more than 1,600 employees located in 23 offices on three continents, with more LEED Accredited Professionals than any design firm. We hold a common philosophy and standard of excellence, and our firm shares expertise across offices worldwide. This inclusive strategy focuses us on our clients, our communities and our vision, which is as compelling today as it was at the firm's inception: to craft ideas + buildings that honor the broader goals of society.

ACKNOWLEDGEMENTS

/ INTRODUCTION /

Photography: Welcome Letter (002); Ron Wu Photography

Forward written by Phil Harrison

/ PERKINS+WILL HISTORICAL ARTIFACTS /

Photography: Bill Brubaker Sketch (010-011), courtesy of Perkins+Will / Photos (048-049), Perkins+Will, courtesy of Terry Owens / Books (098-099), Cocking, Walter D. and Lawrence B. Perkins, *Schools,* Progressive Architecture Library © 1949; Perkins, Fellows and Hamilton Architects, *Educational Buildings,* Perkins, Fellows and Hamilton, © 1925; Perkins, Lawrence B., *Workplace for Learning,* Reinhold Publishing Corporation, © 1957; Ron Wu Photography

/ COLLABORATION + MODERNISM /

Photography: Heathcote Elementary School (012-013); Hedrich-Blessing Photography / Stamford Hospital (016-017); Bill Rothschild Photography

/ PERKINS+WILL LEADERSHIP /

Video Captures: Phil Harrison (006-007) / Ralph Johnson (020-021) / Peter Busby (058-059) / Eileen Jones (108-109) / Eva Maddox (150-151); About Face Media

/ EDUCATION COMES TO ITS SENSES /

Illustration: Crow Island Diagram (023); Perkins+Will / Photography: Crow Island (024-025); Hedrich-Blessing Photography / (026-027); About Face Media and 50,000feet

/ SPROUT SPACE /

Client: DeKalb County Schools

ATLANTA / Project Team: Allen Post, John Poelker, Shawn Hamlin, Jack Allin, Joe Jamgochian, Sumegha Shah, Erika Morgan / 3D Modeling and Visualization: Erika Morgan

Photography: Students Working (028-029); ableimages/Getty Images / Portable Classroom (030-031); Tom H. Johnson, Jr., Pine Mountain, GA / Blue Sky (034-035); French/Getty Images / Artist/Photographer: Blackboard (038-039); Alanna Risse / Illustrations: (040-045, 047); Erika Morgan

/ SUSTAINABILITY + TRUST /

Photography: National College of Agriculture (050-051); courtesy of Perkins+Will / Skybridge (054-055); James Steinkamp Photography

/ ARLINGTON FREE CLINIC /

Client: Arlington Free Clinic

WASHINGTON, DC / Design and Managing Principal: Tama Duffy Day / Project Architect: Jonathan Hoffschneider / Project Designer: Jamie Huffcut / Design Team: Rachel Conrad, Matthew DeGeeter, Lori Geftic / Technical Review: Richard Adams, Marian Danowski

General Contractor: Bognet Construction Associates, Inc. / Engineering & Commissioning: Integral Group / Furniture Dealer: Washington Workplace, Inc.

Photography: Crowd (060-061); Pat McDermott / Research Wall (064-065); Ron Wu Photography / Volunteers (070); Matthew J. DeGeeter / Architectural Photography (071-077); Ken Hayden Photography

/ VANDUSEN BOTANICAL GARDEN /

Client: Vancouver Parks Board

VANCOUVER / Design Director: Peter Busby / Project Architect: Jim Huffman / Design Team: Harley Grusko, Penny Martyn, Paul Cowcher, Robin Glover, Jacqueline Ho, Matthieu Lemay

Structural Consultants: Fast + Epp / Mechanical Consultants: Cobalt Engineering / Electrical Consultants: Cobalt Engineering / Cost Consultants: BTY Group / Code Consultants: B.R. Thorson Ltd. / Envelope Consultant: Morrison Herschfield / Acoustics: BKL Consultants / Landscape Architect: Cornelia Oberlander with Sharp + Diamond Landscape Architecture

Photography: Flower Petals (078-079); Wasserman/Getty Images / Rain Water (082-083); Nacivet/Getty Images / Illustrations: (080-081); Jim Huffman, (086-087, 090-095); Harley Grusko

/ CREATIVITY + EVOLUTION /

Photography: Edens Theater (100-101); Hedrich-Blessing Photography / The International Terminal at O'Hare International Airport (104-105); Hedrich-Blessing Photography

+↗

/ BELTLINE CORRIDOR DESIGN /

Client: The Atlanta BeltLine Inc.

ATLANTA / Managing Principal: Leo Alvarez / Design Manager & Senior
Urban Designer: Ryan Gravel / Project Manager & Senior Urban Designer:
John Threadgill / Transportation Planner: Heather Alhadeff / Senior Urban
Designer: David Green / Urban Designers: Kevin Bacon, Cassie Branum,
Chad Stacy / Urban Designer II: Jeff Williams / Senior Landscape Architect:
Valdis Zusmanis / Landscape Architect: Maxine Coleman, Justin Cooper,
Micah Lipscomb, Zan Stewart / Landscape Architect I: Zhen Feng,
Matt Malone, Xue Phyllis Zhou

CHICAGO / Design Principal: Eva Maddox / Global BE Discipline Leader:
Eileen Jones / BE Senior Project Manager: Tom Boeman / BE Project Manager:
Lisa Coghlan Dolan / BE Designer II: Kimberly Lindstrom / BE Designer II:
Lynette Klein / BE Designer II: Pamela Steiner / Intern: Sara Ahrns

VANCOUVER / Principal: Martin Nielsen / Intermediate Architect: Aaron Knorr

Landscape Architecture, Urban Design: James Corner Field Operations /
Lead Engineer (Civil, Structural, Environmental) & Surveyor: MACTEC
Engineering and Consulting / Engineer & Surveyor: B&E Jackson Associates /
Roadway Engineer & Surveyor: Street Smarts / Surveyor: Agility Surveying Co.,
Inc. / Transit Engineer: HDR / Supporting Landscape Architect: Pond/Ecos /
Sustainability Engineer: Buro Happold / Public Realm Operations &
Management Strategist: HR&A Advisors / Ecologist: Biohabitats / Historic
Preservation Architect: Lord, Aeck & Sargent Architecture / Cultural Historian:
Morrison Design, LLC / Lighting Designer: Leni Schwendinger Light Projects /
Art Advisor: Danielle Roney, LLC / Public Realm Operations & Maintenance
Consultant: BCN Consulting / Cost Estimator: Costing Services Group, Inc. /
Community Engagement Consultant: Panache Communications /
Civil Engineer: Kimley-Horn and Associates, Inc.

Photography: Aerial Images (118-119, 122-123); © Google Earth /
Systems Analysis Diagram (124-125); Ron Wu Photography / Illustrations:
(128-129); Perkins+Will/James Corner Field Operations

/ WHITESPACE.BZ /

Client: The Dixie Group

CHICAGO / Design Principal: Eileen Jones / Brand Strategist: Brian
Weatherford / Project Manager: Nicole Pallante / Project Designer: K.J. Kim /
Designers: Lynette Klein, Elizabeth Mohl, Kayo Takasugi

Website Development: IBM / Webisodes: Radar Studios

Photography: Charrette Materials (130-131) / Carpet Samples (138-139, 148) /
Print Collateral (142-143); Ron Wu Photography / "Ephemera" (136-137);
Mark Laita Photography / Computer Screen (140-141); 50,000feet

/ STUDENT OF THE WORLD /

Client: King Saud bin Abdulaziz University for Health Sciences; Saudi Arabia
National Guard Health Affairs

MULTIPLE OFFICES / Managing Principal: Jones Lindgren / Design Principals:
Jimmy Smith (Riyadh), Nick Seierup (Jeddah), Andy Clinch (al Hasa) /
Interiors: Amy Sickeler, Jo Carmen / Landscape: Leo Alvarez / Planning
Principals: Bob Lavey, Bill Nation, Dan Watch, Dede Woodring / Project
Manager: John Elvin / Branded Environments: Eileen Jones

Project Management and Engineering: Dar Al-Handasah (Shair and Partners) /
Engineering Concept Design and Energy Modeling: Integral Group

Illustrations: (153-155); Perkins+Will/Dar Al-Handasah (Shair and Partners)

/ WORKS CITED /

Cocking, Walter D. and Lawrence B. Perkins, *Schools*, Progressive Architecture
Library, © 1949 / Perkins, Fellows and Hamilton Architects, *Educational
Buildings*, Perkins, Fellows and Hamilton, © 1925 / Perkins, Lawrence B.,
Workplace for Learning, Reinhold Publishing Corporation, © 1957. / Perkins &
Will, *Perkins & Will: The First Fifty Years* / Shair, Kamal A., *Out of the Middle East:
The Emergence of an Arab Global Business*, New York: I.B. Tauris & Co. Ltd.,
© 2006 / *Oral history of C. William Brubaker*. Interviewed by Betty J. Blum,
compiled under the auspices of the Chicago Architects Oral History Project,
Ernest R. Graham Study Center for Architectural Drawings, Department of
Architecture, the Art Institute of Chicago. © 2000 / *Oral history of Lawrence
Bradford Perkins, F.A.I.A.* Interviewed by Betty J. Blum, compiled under
the auspices of the Chicago Architects Oral History Project, Department of
Architecture, the Art Institute of Chicago. © 2000 / Schneider, Mark,
Do School Facilities Affect Academic Outcomes?, National Clearinghouse
for Educational Facilities, © 2002

/ IDEAS + BUILDINGS, VOLUME .03 /

Editor: 50,000feet
Design: 50,000feet

Published: Perkins+Will, Inc.
Printed: Sandy Alexander, Clifton, NJ

Paper: Mohawk Options, 100% PC White, smooth (80# text, 130# dtc)

/ ACKNOWLEDGEMENTS /

Thank you to all who contributed to this important publication and to
the Perkins+Will Ideas + Buildings, Volume .03 team including Phil Harrison,
Katie Overbaugh, Roshelle Born and especially Bill Viehman, a tireless
champion of history who taught us that 75 years is just the beginning.

WE HAVE CREATED THE LARGEST SUSTAINABLE DESIGN FIRM IN THE WORLD.

This piece is printed on process-chlorine free FSC™-certified paper. The FSC principles and criteria include conserving biological diversity, conserving old growth forests, protecting the well-being of indigenous groups and slowing global climate change. Mohawk Options PC100 is made with 100% post-consumer recycled fiber, 100% certified renewable electricity, and is Green Seal™ Certified.

RECYCLED
Paper made from recycled material
FSC® C020268

The savings achieved by choosing PC recycled fiber in place of virgin fiber:

144

TREES PRESERVED FOR THE FUTURE

416

LBS. WATER-BORNE-WASTE NOT GENERATED

61,137

GALLONS WASTE WATER FLOW SAVED

6,764

LBS. SOLID WASTE NOT GENERATED

13,319

NET GREENHOUSE GASES PREVENTED

101,945,600

BTUs ENERGY NOT CONSUMED

Additional savings from using wind-generated electricity are equivalent to:

153

TREES PLANTED

1,960

MILES NOT DRIVEN

IDEAS + BUILDINGS

Perkins+Will : Ideas + Buildings
Space to Place / 75 Years of Design Innovation

Copyright © 2010 Perkins+Will, Inc. All rights reserved.
www.perkinswill.com

ISBN: 978-0-9815436-2-8